CAR-SIZED CRABS

AND OTHER ANIMAL GIANTS

Published 2013 by
A&C Black
An imprint of Bloomsbury Publishing Plc
50 Bedford Square, London, WC1B 3DP

www.bloomsbury.com

ISBN HB 978-1-4081-8183-6
ISBN PB 978-1-4081-9481-2

A CIP catalogue for this book is available from the British Library.

All photographs © Shutterstock, except: p23 (inset) John Sparks/naturepl.com; p31 (inset) © Gerard Soury/Oxford Scientific/Getty Images; p37 (inset) © Brandon Cole/naturepl.com; p38 (inset) © Citron; p38 © Christian Darkin/Science Photo Library; p39 (inset) Y23; p40 © Doug Perrine/naturepl.com; p41 (inset) © Jeff Rotman/naturepl.com; p44 © Scubazoo/Science Photo Library; p44 (inset) © Jany Sauvenet/ Science Photo Library; p46 © Doug Allan/naturepl.com; p48 © Nick Upton/naturepl.com; p55 (inset) © Damian Herde / Shutterstock.com; p60 (inset) © J. Patrick Fischer; p61 © Tom McHugh/Science Photo Library; p62 © Daniel Heuclin/naturepl.com; p63 (inset) © ANDREW MURRAY/naturepl.com; p72 © PETER REESE/naturepl; p73 © Mark Carwardine/naturepl.com; p74 (inset) and p74 © Jabruson/naturepl. com; p76 © François Gilson / Biosphoto / steveblooom.com; p77 (inset) © Bristol City Museum/naturepl. com; p78 © Nature Production/naturepl.com; p79 (inset) Scott Camazine/Science Photo Library; p80 © Pete Oxford/naturepl.com; p81 (inset) © Julio.ospinao; p82 (inset) © Snakecollector; p83 © Morkelsker; p84 (inset) © Tony Heald/naturepl.com; p85 © Jabruson/naturepl; p88 © Natural History Museum, London/Science Photo Library; p89 © Fir0002; p91 (inset) © Charlie Summers/naturepl.com.

Printed in China by Toppan Leefung.

HB 10 9 8 7 6 5 4 3 2
PB 10 9 8 7 6 5 4 3 2 1

CAR-SIZED CRABS

AND OTHER ANIMAL GIANTS

WRITTEN BY

Anna Claybourne

A & C BLACK

AN IMPRINT OF BLOOMSBURY

LONDON NEW DELHI NEW YORK SYDNEY

CONTENTS

Slithery and slimy giants

Big birds

Giant creepy-crawlies

A WORLD OF GIANTS

In our everyday lives, we humans are used to feeling quite large. Unless you're a farmer or a zookeeper, you're probably bigger than most of the creatures you usually come across, like bees and flies, garden birds, mice, or pet cats and dogs. In fact, we are much bigger than most of the other species on the planet, as there are so many types of tiny bugs and creepy-crawlies.

FACT FILES

For each giant creature in this book, check out the fact file at the bottom of the page for vital statistics, interesting facts, and a size comparison so you can see how you might measure up to these incredible beasts.

THE BIGGEST OF THE SMALL

However, not all of the giants you'll meet in this book are bigger than you. It's equally amazing to see a huge version of a creature that you expect to be tiny – like a monster hairy spider, wasp, worm, crab or deep-sea woodlouse. You'll also find out about all of these record-breaking not-so-minibeasts on the following pages.

GIANTS OF THE PAST

Far back in the Earth's history, many types of animals grew much bigger than they do today. There were super-sized sharks, penguins, sloths, dragonflies and hippos, as well as dozens of types of mighty dinosaurs. However, none of them, as far as we know, could beat the biggest creature of all time, the blue whale, which still roams the world to this day (see page 24).

CLOSE UP
A photographer has an exciting encounter with a whale shark.

MEETING A MONSTER

Whether you're meeting an elephant, a whale, a towering giraffe or a powerful big cat, it's such an incredible sight, you want to get closer and take a better look, yet your instincts are telling you to run!

AFRICAN ELEPHANT

The African elephant is the biggest land animal in the world. So how big is it? A large male is 3-4m tall and 6-7m long – so big, he wouldn't fit into most people's front rooms. One large elephant weighs the same as about 200 human 10-year-olds!

MIGHTY MONSTERS

Elephants are incredibly strong. They can push trees over by leaning on them, in order to eat all the leaves, or pick up heavy logs with their trunks. They can run pretty fast, thundering along at up to 40km/h. But they can be delicate and careful too. The tip of an elephant's trunk is so sensitive, it can use it to pick up a peanut, or grab a single blade of grass.

DID YOU KNOW?
African elephants are good swimmers, and can use their trunks as snorkels!

UNDERGROUND SOUND
Elephants talk by trumpeting and growling to each other. They also make a deep rumbling sound that makes the ground vibrate. Other elephants can sense the vibrations up to 10km away.

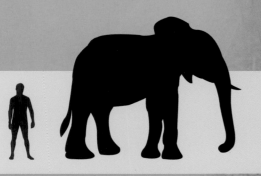

MAXIMUM SIZE: 4.2m tall **MAXIMUM WEIGHT:** 12,000kg
FOUND IN: African grasslands and bush
CREATURE FEATURE: 2m-long trunk with two small finger-like parts at the tip.

ELEPHANT FACE
Elephants are unmistakeable, with their trunks, tusks and huge, flappy ears. The elephant's trunk is made of its upper lip and nose joined together, and its tusks are two of its front teeth.

GENTLE GIANTS?

African elephants live in family groups, led by a mother or grandmother elephant. All the adults help to look after and protect the babies. So people often think of elephants as kind, clever and calm. But watch out! Elephants can turn nasty, especially young males, or mothers who have a baby. And when they do, it can be very dangerous. A ginormous, grumpy elephant charging towards you could squash you as flat as a pancake!

RHINOCEROS

In Portugal, almost 500 years ago, a rhinoceros stepped off a boat from India, and caused a sensation. People in Europe had heard of rhinos, but thought they were mythical beasts. They were amazed when a real live one turned up, with its amazing nose-horn, armour-thick skin, and ENORMOUS size!

RHINOS OF THE WORLD

This rhino, named Ganda, was an Indian or greater one-horned rhinoceros. They can reach almost 4m long and 2m tall, and weigh as much as a minibus. But they aren't the biggest rhinos! That title goes to the African white rhino. A male can grow to 4.5m long, and weigh as much as 4,000kg. Its massive head alone can be a metre long, and so can its front horn.

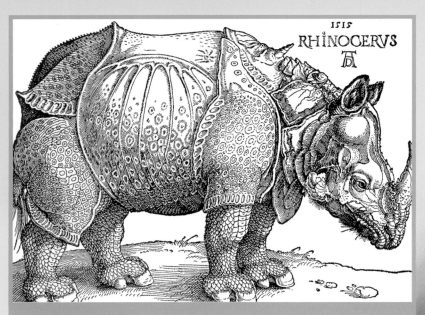

1515
RHINOCERVS

RHINO ON RECORD

Artist Albrecht Dürer engraved this famous portrait of Ganda the rhino after hearing about him. The description above the picture includes the words:
'In size it is like the elephant, but shorter in the legs and very much prepared for fighting. It has a sharp strong horn on the front of the nose, which it sharpens on stones. It is a triumphant animal, the elephants' deadly enemy.'

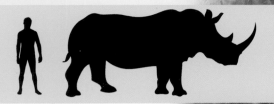

MAXIMUM SIZE: 4.5m long **MAXIMUM WEIGHT:** 4,000kg
FOUND IN: Grasslands, swamps and forests in India, southeast Asia and Africa **CREATURE FEATURE:** One or two nose horns, made of a hard fingernail-like substance.

CHAAAAAARRGE!

Like many animal giants, rhinos are plant-eating vegetarians. They like wandering around, grazing on grass, and rolling in mud. However, this doesn't mean they're not dangerous. If they're angry they can charge at you, thundering along at over 50km/h with their sharp horns at the ready. Black rhinos are especially bad-tempered, and often die in fights with other rhinos. Don't get in their way!

DID YOU KNOW?

Tales of the mythical unicorn, a horse with a horn on its nose, may have started when ancient travellers described rhinos. The rhino is the only land animal with a nose horn.

HIPPOPOTAMUS

After elephants and rhinos, the hippopotamus is the third largest animal on land. Hippos' huge, chubby, rounded bodies and stumpy legs can make them seem cute and comical. In cartoons, they're often shown as lazy, harmless creatures who just wallow in mud. But if you live in Africa, the hippo's home, this is the large animal you fear the most.

MUNCH!

Hippos usually weigh a bit less than the biggest rhinos, but they can grow longer – up to 5m from nose to tail. This is partly because of their enormous heads and jaws. A hippo has a HUGE mouth, which it can open incredibly wide, revealing its terrifyingly long, sharp teeth. Some hippos have teeth as long as your arm! They mainly feed on grass, but use their teeth for fighting each other, or mauling anyone who annoys them.

DID YOU KNOW?

Though hippos are similar in size to rhinos, and look a bit like giant pigs, their closest relatives are actually whales!

KEEP OFF MY PATCH!
Hippos like to be able to get into the water quickly at any time, so getting between a hippo and its river home can make it extremely mad.

MAXIMUM SIZE: 5.5m long **MAXIMUM WEIGHT:** 3,000kg
FOUND IN: African rivers **CREATURE FEATURE:** Huge mouth and very long, razor-sharp teeth.

HIPPOS ON TIPTOES

The name 'hippopotamus' means 'river horse', and hippos spend most of their time in rivers. The water supports their bulky bodies, so they can prance along, glide and leap like ballet dancers while underwater.

It's also in water that hippos are most deadly. They guard their own section of river fiercely, and attack any other animal, boat or human that gets too close. With its mighty mouth, a hippo can slice a boat or a person completely in two. They can run fast on land as well and and have been known to chase people at high speed.

FLYING FOX

Spread out your arms as wide as you can. Your armspan is similar to the wingspan of the large flying fox – which is not actually a fox at all, but the world's biggest bat. Maybe you thought bats like that only existed as Halloween decorations, or in vampire films! But bats this big really are out there.

FURRY FACES

Flying foxes get their name because their pointy, furry faces resemble a fox. They are also known as megabats. There are many flying fox species, and they vary in size – but the large flying fox, Livingstone's flying fox, black flying fox and Indian flying fox are all enormous.

Most of their size comes from their wide wings, made of skin stretched between long, spindly finger bones. Their furry bodies are closer to the size of a cat or a small monkey. To stay in the air, flying foxes must also be very light, so they only weigh around a kilo – as much as a small bunch of bananas.

MONSTER MOMENT

According to folklore, an even bigger bat, the mysterious Ahool, roams the forests of Java in southeast Asia. It's said to cry 'a-HOO-oool!' as it flies through the night, and has a reported wingspan of over 3m – twice as big as the biggest flying foxes. Yikes! However, there's no evidence so far that it really exists.

MAXIMUM SIZE: 1.5m wingspan **MAXIMUM WEIGHT:** 1.2kg **FOUND IN:** India, Asia, Australia and islands around Africa. **CREATURE FEATURE:** Huge, spreading, leathery wings, attached to the bat's arms and fingers.

FRUIT FAN

Some bats eat insects, some eat fish or frogs, and some, the vampire bats, really do sneak up and suck people's blood. Luckily for us, flying foxes don't do that. They feed on fruit and nectar from flowers, giving them another of their names, 'giant fruit bat'.

HANGING AROUND
When it stops for a rest, a flying fox hangs upside down by its feet, like other bats, and wraps its wings around itself.

TIGER

The tiger is the **biggest cat in the world**. In body shape, a tiger is a bit like a pet cat (a very muscly, stripy one!) – but MUCH more massive. The biggest tigers, from Siberia in Russia, can reach 3.3m long, including their tails, and weigh 300kg.

POUNCE!

Besides being big, tigers are super-strong, with massive jaw muscles for crunching bones, and powerful legs for jumping. Think how easily a pet cat can leap up onto a fence. A tiger can leap like that, but 5m high! Leaping along the ground, it can jump even further. Tigers hunt by jumping – they sneak up on prey until they are close enough, then POUNCE!

WILL IT EAT ME?

Tigers can jump so high, they've sometimes escaped from zoo enclosures. Humans aren't their favourite food (they prefer wild pigs and deer) but they have been known to attack and eat people, both in zoos and in the wild.

DID YOU KNOW?
Unlike most pet cats, tigers love baths. They splash and cool off in rivers, ponds and even the sea.

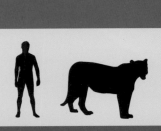

MAXIMUM SIZE: 3.3m long **MAXIMUM WEIGHT:** 300kg **FOUND IN:** East and southeast Asia **CREATURE FEATURE:** Each tiger has its own unique pattern of black and orange stripes.

THE WHAT?

Actually, there is one cat that's bigger than a tiger – the liger!
A liger is a big cat with a lion dad, and a tiger mum. Ligers
don't really count, because they don't exist in the wild, as lions
and tigers live in different parts of the world. They are only
bred in captivity. But for some reason, they grow enormous.
One famous liger, Hercules, weighs over 500kg and measures
almost 4m – as long as a car!

BIG BITE
After pouncing on its prey, a tiger
uses its jaws to kill it, with a
powerful bite on the neck or head.

GIRAFFE

There's no mistaking a giraffe. Nothing else on Earth looks like this toweringly tall tree-muncher. It's the tallest animal in the world, growing to almost 6m. That means if you looked out of a window two floors up, you could be just about face-to-face with a giraffe!

IT'S ALL LONG

Giraffes are famous for their long necks – a male giraffe's neck on its own can be around 2.5m long, taller than most men. But they also have very, very long legs, which help them to gallop across the plains of Africa, where they live. Even giraffes' rubbery tongues are 45-50cm long. They curl them around tree branches, then pull to strip off the leaves.

HELLO UP THERE!

Why are they so lanky? Giraffes have adapted over time to suit a diet of juicy treetop leaves. The taller they are, the easier it is for them to find food. Being so tall also helps them spot danger on the horizon, such as a hungry lion on the prowl.

SLURP!
The giraffe's stretchy, bendy tongue is a perfect tool for collecting all the tasty leaves from a tree branch.

MAXIMUM SIZE: 5.8m **MAXIMUM WEIGHT:** 1.900kg **FOUND IN:** African grasslands, scrub and woodlands **CREATURE FEATURE:** The giraffe's huge, thick and super-strong neck is unique in the animal kingdom.

DID YOU KNOW?
Male giraffes fight by whacking each other with their heads and necks. Sometimes a giraffe gets knocked out and topples to the ground!

HIGH AND LOW
Males are taller and reach for the tops of trees, while females feed lower down.

GORILLA

Gorillas are the biggest animals in the primate family, which includes apes and monkeys. It also includes us, which might be why we find gorillas so fascinating. They look very like us, and often seem to make human-like facial expressions.

HOW BIG?

A large male gorilla can stand up 1.8m tall, similar to a tall person. However, gorillas are MUCH broader and stronger than humans, weighing up to 200kg, or three times as much as an average man. Their chests are huge and barrel-shaped, and their arms are longer and stronger than their legs. A large male gorilla can stretch his arms almost 3m wide.

MONSTER MOMENT

In 1979, TV naturalist David Attenborough was welcomed into a wild gorilla troop while filming in Rwanda, Africa. They groomed him and snuggled up to him! He remarked:
'There is more meaning and mutual understanding in exchanging a glance with a gorilla than with any other animal I know.'

SCARY MONSTERS?

Thanks to some cartoons and films that show gorillas as terrifying monsters, we think of them as fierce, chest-beating beasts. In fact, they are very gentle – much less fierce than their cousins the chimpanzees. Gorillas are vegetarians, and love lounging around in a family group, nibbling leaves, grunting and grooming each other. Male gorillas do beat their chests, though – they do this to make a noise and scare other gorillas away from their family.

MAXIMUM SIZE: 1.8m tall **MAXIMUM WEIGHT:** 220kg **FOUND IN:** African forests
CREATURE FEATURE: Older males are called silverbacks, as they grow silvery-grey hair on their backs and legs.

GORILLA CUDDLE
A young gorilla stretches out on David Attenborough for a rest.

SCARY TEETH
Older male gorillas have sharp fangs, which they use for fighting each other.

WHALE SHARK

Is it a shark? Is it a whale? Is it a strange, speckled submarine? The whale shark is, in fact, a shark – the biggest shark in the world, which also makes it the world's biggest fish. It can grow up to around 12m from snout to tail, which is the length of an average bus. There are reports of much bigger whale sharks too, some as big as 18m long. Scientists have never recorded one that huge, but that doesn't mean they're not out there...

GENTLE GIANT

Its amazing size doesn't mean this shark
is a terrifying, sharp-toothed man-eater. In fact,
like some other super-sized sharks, the basking shark and
the megamouth, the whale shark only eats small prey. It's a filter-feeder,
cruising along slowly, gulping gallons of water into its mouth, which is as
wide as a small sofa, and sieving out small fish and plankton. Whale sharks
are also known for being gentle and friendly to humans.

MAXIMUM SIZE: 12m long **MAXIMUM WEIGHT:** 20,000 kg **FOUND IN:** Warm, tropical seas around the equator **CREATURE FEATURE:** Massive mouth up to 1.5m across.

HITCHING A RIDE

As a whale shark swims along, it will often have smaller fish called remoras clinging to its tail or underside. The remoras have sucker-like mouths for holding on, and feed on the shark's poo! Some whale sharks have even been known to let human divers hang onto them and go for a ride too.

CLING-ONS
Remoras don't just cling to whale sharks. They are also found on other sharks, whales and turtles.

SPOTTED SHARKS
Whale sharks have unusual spotted and striped skin markings and very wide, flat heads and mouths.

MONSTER MOMENT
In 2011, an underwater photographer was filming whale sharks in Mexico when one came so close, he almost got sucked into its mouth. However, although they have massive mouths, whale sharks have small throats, and couldn't actually swallow a human.

GREAT WHITE SHARK

The great white shark is an animal giant with a big reputation. Thanks to scary movies, books and horror stories, it's widely regarded as a toothy terror that loves to chase and snap up swimmers, surfers and divers. But is it really such a big, bad monster?

MUNCH!

The great white certainly is a big shark, built for killing large prey. It can reach 6m in length, which is longer than three fully-grown men laid head-to-toe. It has a powerful head and giant jaws, filled with hundreds of razor-sharp, saw-edged teeth. Great whites are also brilliant at tracking down prey: they can sniff blood from 5km away, and have a special electrical sense for detecting the movements of other living things underwater.

TASTY!
This great white is snapping at some meaty bait dangling into the water. Scientists often do this to attract sharks so they can study them.

MAXIMUM SIZE: 6m long Maximum weight: 2,300kg
FOUND IN: Warm seas and oceans around the world, mainly close to coasts. **CREATURE FEATURE:** Hundreds of sharp triangular teeth, some up to 8cm long.

SHARK FOOD

However, if you had a choice between jumping into the water with a great white shark, and jumping into the water with a hippo, you should probably choose the shark. The hippo is more likely to bite you in two (see page 12). Sharks often approach people on the water and check them out, but they rarely eat humans. Experts think they don't really like the taste and texture of human bodies, and usually only attack when they mistake a surfer or swimmer for a tasty seal.

SHARK DIVING
In some places, tourists can go on shark-diving trips and watch tour guides feeding great whites.

DID YOU KNOW?
Great white sharks only kill around 10-20 people around the world each year.

OCEAN SUNFISH

The crazy-looking ocean sunfish's bizarre shape is enough to make you do a double-take. Where's its back end and its tail? It doesn't seem to have them – sometimes giving it the charming nickname 'swimming head'. (It's also called the 'headfish' or 'moonfish'.) What makes it even more unusual is its vast size. This freaky fish grows up to 3m long and 4m in 'finspan', and weighs more than a tonne. In fact it can weigh over two tonnes (2,000kg) and is the third biggest fish in the sea after whale and basking sharks.

FLYING SUNFISH

Sometimes sunfish even right jump out of the water and land on boats – CRASH! This can damage or even sink a small boat, or knock people into the water. But sunfish don't do this deliberately. They are usually curious and friendly around humans, and don't attack them – their favourite food is jellyfish.

MAXIMUM SIZE: 4m across **MAXIMUM WEIGHT:** 2,300kg **FOUND IN:** Tropical and warm seas and oceans. **CREATURE FEATURE:** Unusual body shape, resembling a huge disc with long fins.

ON THE SURFACE

Sunfish get their name because they like to lie flat on the sea surface, sunning themselves. No one is sure why, but it could be a way of warming up their bodies after going on a deep dive. Because of this habit, sunfish sadly often get caught in fishing nets meant for other fish, and are sometimes crashed into by boats. (Which is bad news for the fish AND the boats!)

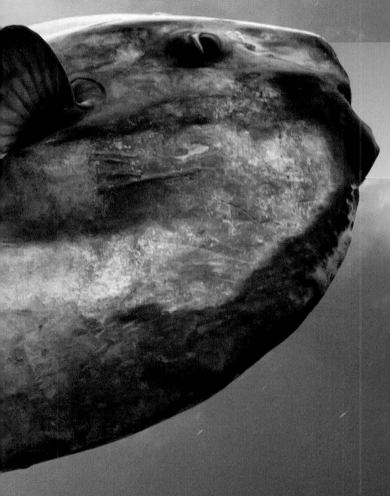

SEA MONSTER
This sunfish is so massive, its body is bigger than a double bed. To grow this big, sunfish have to eat a LOT of jellyfish.

DID YOU KNOW?
The ocean sunfish holds the record for most eggs laid at once – 300 million!

WHAT'S THAT!?
As it relaxes near the surface to soak up some rays, one of the sunfish's fins sticks out of the water. People sometimes see this and mistake the sunfish for a shark.

COLOSSAL AND GIANT SQUID

Two types of
monster squid
are known to roam
the dark, chilly ocean
depths – the giant squid,
and the colossal squid. But
which is the biggest?

LONG AND LANKY

The giant squid is thought to be the longest, with a total
length (including its extra-long tentacles) of up to 13m.
(Some reports say 18m, but scientists say it's possible
to stretch the tentacles, making these measurements
a bit unreliable.) Giant squid are fierce hunters, and the
suckers on their tentacles are ringed with saw-like teeth.

BROAD AND BULKY

The colossal squid has a much bigger
body, or mantle, than the giant squid, as
well as bigger fins and a bigger head,
but shorter arms and tentacles. Experts
think colossal squid are slow movers
who wait for their prey, instead
of chasing it. They have swivelling
hooks on their tentacles to help them
grab fish and other squid.

MAXIMUM SIZE: 12-13m **MAXIMUM WEIGHT:** 900kg **FOUND IN:** Cold or deep
oceans. **CREATURE FEATURE:** Eight arms, like an octopus, plus two extra-long
grabbing tentacles.

MYSTERIES OF THE DEEP

Both these squid are quite mysterious – they are rarely spotted alive. Most of what we know about them comes from bits of dead squid that get washed up, caught in fishing nets, or found in other sea creatures' stomachs.

STINKY SQUID
Scientists often study old, dead squid like this one, but they are often rotten or have bits missing.

THE SQUID AND THE WHALE

Sperm whales (see page 26) hunt both giant and colossal squid. The squid often fight back, so sperm whales can be left with sucker-shaped scars on their bodies.

DID YOU KNOW?
Giant and colossal squid have the biggest eyes on Earth. Each of their eyeballs is bigger than your head!

CAUGHT ON CAMERA
Giant squid were first filmed alive and in the wild as recently as 2004.

LION'S MANE JELLYFISH

Imagine going for a swim and bumping into this! You could get lost under its flappy fringes and tangled up in its trailing, spaghetti-like tentacles. Ugh! What IS it?

GIANT JELLY

It's the lion's mane jellyfish, the biggest jellyfish in the world. This enormous, brainless blob can grow to 2.2m across, with tentacles 30m long. That's so big that 10 divers could sit underneath it (if all those tentacles, frilly flaps and dangly bits weren't in the way).

BLOBBING ALONG
Like other jellyfish, the lion's mane usually just drifts around, waiting for prey to swim into its grasp.

MAXIMUM SIZE: 2.2m across **MAXIMUM LENGTH:** 30m
FOUND IN: Mainly northern seas and oceans, but also around Australia and New Zealand. **CREATURE FEATURE:** Long, stinging tentacles that trail through the water.

HEEEELP!

Don't panic – the lion's mane jelly isn't quite as dangerous as it looks. It is a hunter, and stings prey such as fish with its tentacles before eating them up. But its sting isn't deadly; it's more like a bee sting. It also eats very slowly, so even if you did get stuck in one, you'd have time to get away. There are no records of these jellyfish gobbling up humans.

LURKING LION
In this photo, you can see a boat and a diver from beneath the waves, with a lion's mane lurking below them.

MONSTER MOMENT
You might see photos of divers with lion's mane jellyfish that look not just huge, but absolutely humungous! But these photos are fake, or sometimes make the diver look close-up when actually he or she is far away. Don't worry – the lion's mane jelly does NOT reach the size of a house.

LEATHERBACK TURTLE

We usually think of turtles as smallish animals that can live in tanks as pets. Bigger ones are found in the sea, of course – but just how big can a turtle be? The leatherback holds the record, and it's massive. Its giant, bendy, leathery shell can measure over 2.2m, and it can grow to over 3m in total length. It's a turtle the size of a small car!

SLOW CRAWL

In the sea, the water supports the leatherback's weight, letting it swim freely. But when females crawl ashore to lay their eggs in the sand, they have to drag themselves along slowly. If they were any bigger, they probably couldn't move on land at all.

SANDY NEST
A female leatherback uses her flippers to scoop out a nest in the sandy beach to lay her eggs in.

MAXIMUM SIZE: 3m long **MAXIMUM WEIGHT:** 900kg **FOUND IN:** Most of the world's seas and oceans, especially in warmer areas.
CREATURE FEATURE: Its unique shell, which is flexible and feels like thick leather or rubber.

RECORD BREAKER

Leatherbacks aren't just the biggest turtles – they're the oldest, most wide-ranging and swim the deepest too.

- They've been around for 150 million years, predating many of the dinosaurs.
- They can dive 1,200m deep, deeper than any other turtle.
- They have the longest turtle flippers, over a metre long.
- They migrate long distances to feed and breed, covering as much as 16,000km in a year.

SMOOTH SWIMMER
The leatherback's shell is a streamlined shape with ridges along it, to help the turtle glide through the water easily.

TURTLE TEARS

Leatherbacks sometimes appear to cry turtle tears, but it's actually just their way of getting extra sea salt out of their bodies.

DID YOU KNOW?

Leatherback turtles feed mainly on jellyfish. They can die from accidentally eating floating plastic bags in the sea because they look like jellyfish.

GIANT ISOPOD

Look under a stone in your garden or local park, and you'll probably find a woodlouse (also called a slater, pillbug, sowbug or chuggypig!). Some people don't like them very much, but at least they're only little – no more than 2cm long. But far away, at the bottom of the sea, lives the woodlouse's monstrous cousin, the giant isopod.

AAAAARRGGGH!

The giant isopod is far from being the biggest animal in this book, but it might win the prize for the scariest-looking. It's like a huge, white woodlouse the size of a dog, with enormous spiky claws and a face like an alien robot. Bet you're glad this doesn't live in your garden!

MAXIMUM SIZE: 75cm long **MAXIMUM WEIGHT:** 1.7kg **FOUND ON:** The deep ocean floor **CREATURE FEATURE:** Glittering, triangular compound eyes, each made up of 4,000 lenses.

YUM YUM!

Like their land-living relatives, giant isopods are scavengers and feed mainly on dead, decaying plants and animals. They might sometimes catch themselves a slow-moving fish or a sea worm, but they don't tend to bite or attack people. Phew!

MINI COUSIN
You can see quite a few similarities between a tiny common woodlouse and its deep-sea giant relative.

DID YOU KNOW?
Woodlice aren't insects – they are crustaceans, like crabs, prawns and lobsters, as well as the giant isopod. Most of their relatives live in the sea.

BOOTLACE WORM

The bootlace worm doesn't sound like a very large animal, and in some ways it's not. You could walk past one hiding in a rock pool at the beach, and not notice it at all. But this humble worm holds an amazing record – it's the longest animal on our planet. Longer than the biggest snakes. Longer than a blue whale, the biggest animal on Earth. Longer than the longest dinosaur that ever lived.

LONG AND SKINNY
Though they're very long, bootlace worms are usually only about 1cm wide, but they can be thicker.

MAXIMUM SIZE: 55m long **FOUND IN:** Shallow seas and seashores in northern Europe **CREATURE FEATURE:** Slime glands for covering itself in a slippery, gloopy coating.

AS LONG AS A VERY LONG PIECE OF STRING

The bootlace worm's scientific name is *Lineus longissimus*. Sounds complicated, but it's actually Latin for 'very long piece of string' – because that's what this worm looks like. It's brownish, thin, and likes to lie in a coiled-up, tangled heap in rock pools, or on the shallow seabed. It's only when you unravel it and lay it out in a line that you can see its incredible length.

MONSTER MOMENT

The bootlace worm is mostly harmless, but if you try to pick it up, you'll get covered in handfuls of slippery, smelly slime! The worm releases it to help it escape if a predator grabs it. The slime also helps it slither around without getting stuck in a knot or scraping itself on rocks.

LONGEST WORM EVER

Not all bootlace worms are super-long – they're often only about 10m (as long as a giant squid). But the longest one on record is thought to have been around 55m long – longer than an Olympic swimming pool. It was found on a beach in St Andrews, Scotland, after a storm, in 1864.

GREEN ANACONDA

If you ever go exploring in the Amazon rainforest, take care as you splash through the streams and steamy swamps. This is where the world's biggest snake can be found, lurking in the shallows, perfectly disguised and ready to pounce.

BIGGEST SNAKE

The green anaconda often stars in jungle adventure films, where it wraps itself around unwary explorers. It's often shown as bigger than its true size. However, even in real life, this is still a massive monster snake. It can reach nearly 9m in length – as long as two large 4x4 cars. But the thing that makes it really monstrous is its thickness. Its body can be 30cm in diameter, or almost a metre around, making it incredibly chunky, powerful and heavy.

MIGHTY COILS
Imagine this wrapping around you and squeezing tight! Anacondas are so strong, there's no way you could escape.

MAXIMUM SIZE: 8.8m long **MAXIMUM WEIGHT:** 230kg **FOUND IN:** Rivers, ponds and swampy areas in northern South America.
CREATURE FEATURE: Eyes and nostrils on top of the head, like a hippo's, let the anaconda hide underwater to wait for passing prey.

OPEN WIDE!

Snakes this big aren't poisonous. Instead, they are 'constrictors'. They coil around their prey and squeeze it so that it can't breathe, then swallow it whole. A green anaconda is big enough to eat a human, and it has been known to happen. Normally, though, they eat fish, lizards and birds, and sometimes larger animals like deer, caimans and capybaras.

WATER SNAKE
Anacondas love water, and are often seen like this, lurking in a shallow pool or pond with their eyes above the surface.

HEY! I'M THE BIGGEST!

The green anaconda is normally awarded the title of biggest snake species, but there's one snake that can grow even longer – the reticulated python. Another constrictor, its world record length is just under 10m.

DID YOU KNOW?
Though they are so big, anacondas are at risk, because they are hunted for their skins, and also to be sold as exotic pets. Who would want one of these as a pet!?

KING COBRA

The king cobra is one of the scariest snakes you could ever bump into. It's much bigger than any other venomous snake, growing up to 5.7m long. Even worse, if it's feeling angry, this snake can stand up and look you in the eye! It can raise up the front part of its body until it's as tall as an adult human, and even in this position it can keep wriggling forwards, ready to strike. Run away!

WATCH OUT!
When it rears up, the cobra flattens and spreads out its neck.

DEADLY BITE

King cobras, like most snakes, are shy, and avoid people if they can. But they will bite if they feel threatened or cornered. Some other snakes have more potent venom, but because king cobras are so big, they inject a lot of poison with each bite. One bite delivers enough to kill up to 30 people, or one elephant – and it works fast, too.

MAXIMUM SIZE: 5.7m long **MAXIMUM WEIGHT:** 14kg **FOUND IN:** India, China and Southeast Asia **CREATURE FEATURE:** The cobra's neck can flare out into a wide hood shape, making it appear even bigger.

MONSTER MOMENT
King cobras don't hiss quietly, like most snakes – instead, they have a low, hissing growl that's said to sound spookily human.

WHO'S BITING WHO?
Cobras like eating other snakes, including venomous ones such as the deadly krait. They seem to be immune to other snakes' venom, so that their bites don't harm them. But another animal, the mongoose, which eats snakes, uses the same trick – cobra venom hardly affects it. It's one of the few creatures that can kill a king cobra, though it usually only attacks very young ones.

DANCING COBRA
Snake charmers sometimes keep cobras and play music for them to 'dance' to. They usually remove the cobra's deadly fangs, though.

SALTWATER CROCODILE

The saltwater crocodile, or 'saltie', is the biggest of all reptiles. Why 'saltwater'? Because besides living in rivers and swamps, this croc hangs out in estuaries (wide river mouths) and even swims out into the open sea. As if sharks and jellyfish aren't enough to worry about, in the seas of south east Asia you could bump into one of these during a swim!

SNAP! SNAP!

Salties have big, strong heads full of muscles to help them bite down hard with their long jaws. To hunt, the croc usually waits in the water, pretending to be a log, until an unfortunate animal (or human) comes for a wash or a drink. Then it suddenly lunges out, grabs its prey, and shakes it violently to and fro, or drags it underwater where it drowns.

RAARRRGGH!
A monster saltie rears up out of the water, showing off its mouthful of massive teeth.

MAXIMUM SIZE: Up to 7m **MAXIMUM WEIGHT:** 1,075kg
FOUND IN: Australia, southeast Asia, India and China,
CREATURE FEATURE: Incredibly long, strong tail for helping the saltie swim fast and lunge out of the water at prey.

HOW BIG?

So just how big can a saltie be? One of the biggest ever measured nearly 7m long, and weighed more than 1,000kg. He was nicknamed Lolong (meaning 'Grandpa'), and was captured in the Philippines in 2011 after being suspected of eating at least two people. He was kept alive, however, and taken to live in captivity in a wildlife park.

SALTIE SNACKS
Mind your fingers! An audience watches saltwater crocodile feeding time at a wildlife park.

MONSTER MOMENT

In 2007, a vet in a zoo in Taiwan was trying to give a poorly crocodile an injection when it turned around and snapped his arm off! Luckily the croc dropped the arm and it was successfully sewn back on.

GIANT TORTOISE

Giant tortoises live in two parts of the world: the Seychelles islands in the Indian Ocean, and the Galapagos Islands in the Pacific. A giant tortoise can grow to 100 times the weight of a smaller species, such as a pet tortoise, weighing over 300kg, with a shell 1.2m long.

SLOW AND STEADY

Like other tortoises, giant tortoises are slow, usually wandering along at well under 1km per hour. They can also reach a great age – the oldest on record are thought to have lived for over 150 years.

IT'S ONLY ME!
On the islands where they live, it's quite normal to see a ginormous tortoise the size of an armchair wandering past.

RUBBER NECK
The giant tortoise's wrinkly neck is very stretchy, making it easier to reach lots of food without having to move much.

TORTOISE MEAT

Giant tortoises can stay safe from most predators by hiding in their huge, heavy shells. But they are no match for hungry humans. In the past, sailors used to stop at the islands, stock up on fresh water, and collect lots of giant tortoises to use as extra-large ready meals. They kept them alive on their ships until they wanted to eat them. Because of this, many types of giant tortoises became extinct, and those that are left are endangered.

MAXIMUM SIZE: 1.5m long **MAXIMUM WEIGHT:** 360kg **FOUND IN:** The Seychelles and Galapagos Islands **CREATURE FEATURE:** Giant tortoises have very long necks, which they can tuck inside their shells, or stretch out to feed on leaves.

EYEWITNESS ACCOUNT

Famous scientist Charles Darwin encountered giant tortoises in the Galapagos. He wrote: 'These huge reptiles, surrounded by the black lava, the leafless shrubs, and large cacti, seemed to my fancy like some antediluvian* animals.' Darwin even tried tortoise-riding!

*Prehistoric

KOMODO DRAGON

CHINESE GIANT SALAMANDER

Meet a truly bizarre water monster – the flat-bodied, fat-toed, beady-eyed, speckly and super-slimy Chinese giant salamander. This is the biggest of the amphibians – the animal family that includes frogs, toads and newts. It's at least a metre long, and some reports say it can reach nearly two metres, the same size as a human.

DARK WATER

You'll rarely spot a giant salamander, even in China. They live in cold, remote mountain streams, where they hide under rocks, or in underwater hollows. They only come out at night, hunting for fish and shrimps to eat. Their tiny eyes are almost useless, and they don't have gills – they breathe directly through their damp skin.

DARK AND DAMP
A Chinese giant salamander on the prowl in its favourite surroundings – a gloomy, rocky river bottom.

ly

MAXIMUM SIZE: 1.8m **MAXIMUM WEIGHT:** 50kg **FOUND IN:** Mountain rivers and streams in parts of China **CREATURE FEATURE:** Special sense organs on the salamander's head let it feel the movement of prey in the water, as it can't see it.

SALAMANDER HUNTING

Though it looks quite scary, this beast is harmless to humans – and in fact it's in great danger, because it has been hunted so much. Hunting giant salamanders is now illegal, but it still happens. People catch them by standing in streams and simply grabbing them, or sometimes by putting poison into the stream, then collecting the dead salamanders. Then, they are sold as a delicacy. To cook a salamander, it's boiled and turned into soup.

DID YOU KNOW?

This salamander makes a strange, spooky noise, which sounds a bit like a dog whimpering or a baby crying. Because of this, in China it has the nickname 'infant fish'.

GOLIATH FROG

If you've ever encountered a frog in the wild, you'll know that when you get too close, it will jump! Frogs have very strong, springy back legs to help them hop out of danger. Even a small frog can startle you with its jumping ability. So how high do you think this monster can leap? The answer is around 3m – much higher than your head!

FOREST FROG

The Goliath frog is massive – it can measure 32cm, or bigger than a football – and that's not including its giant back legs. It lives in the rainforests of west Africa, and is now very rare. Some people keep these frogs as pets, and even have competitions to see which are the best jumpers. However, it's not a good idea to have a pet Goliath frog – they are endangered, and catching and selling them makes this worse.

GIANT JUMPER
A Goliath frog at home in the wild, ready to hop off its rock into the water to go hunting.

MAXIMUM SIZE: 32cm long **MAXIMUM WEIGHT:** 3.5kg **FOUND IN:** West African rainforests
CREATURE FEATURE: Powerful back legs for making monster jumps.

LOOK AT THIS ONE!
In this photo you can see the frog's enormously strong, thick back legs, which make it so good at jumping.

FROG LEG FEAST

The frog's big back legs can cause it problems, as people like to eat them. The large strong leg muscles contain the most tender, tasty meat (for those people who like frog meat!). So these frogs, like many others, are hunted as food, and because of this, they are at risk of dying out.

DID YOU KNOW?

Goliath frogs have very long, sticky tongues to help them grab prey. Their favourite foods include insects, fish and other small water creatures – however, one Goliath frog was found to have gobbled up a bat!

ANDEAN CONDOR

Look at the wingspan on this! As an Andean condor glides and swoops above the Andes mountains of south America, its wings stretch an amazing 3m across. They're the longest wings of any land bird, and carry one of the heaviest flying birds in the world – the biggest condors weigh in at around 15kg.

WIDE WINGS
The splayed feathers on the ends of the condor's wings help it to control its flight.

ON THE GROUND
Sitting down with its wings folded, the condor doesn't look quite as huge, but it's still well over a metre long from head to tail.

MAXIMUM SIZE: 3.2m wingspan **MAXIMUM WEIGHT:** Wingspan
FOUND IN: The Andes mountain range of western South America
CREATURE FEATURE: Males have a red, fleshy comb or crest on their heads, making males and females easy to tell apart.

WHAT IS A CONDOR?

A condor is actually a type of very large vulture. Like most vultures, the Andean condor eats mainly carrion, or dead animals. It glides around searching for dead goats, sheep, seals or llamas on the ground, which it can spot from several kilometres away. Then it swoops down to feed.

DID YOU KNOW?

Vultures such as the condor have bald heads, with no feathers on them. This allows them to nibble right inside the rotting bodies of dead animals, without getting their feather messy. Nice!

HOLLOW BONES

15kg is the same weight as an average human four-year-old, which might not seem like much for such a large animal. But to get off the ground at all, flying birds have to be extremely light. They have hollow bones and feathers, and a beak instead of a jaw and teeth, to keep their bodies as light as possible.

WANDERING ALBATROSS

Here's the bird with the biggest wingspan of all: the wandering albatross of the Southern Ocean. From wingtip to wingtip, it can reach 3.7m. That means each wing is as long as a man is tall.

ON THE WING

The rest of an albatross isn't quite as big and heavy as some other flying birds, and this may help it with its incredible flying feats. Wandering albatrosses are brilliant at staying in the air. After a baby albatross learns to fly, it leaves its nest and spends between five and ten years – yes, years! – at sea, not returning to land at all. It swoops and soars above the ocean, riding on air pushed upwards by the movements of the waves. Sometimes, the albatross will land on the sea to rest, have a drink of seawater, or fish for octopuses and other sea creatures beneath the surface.

DRY LAND AT LAST
Albatrosses do come ashore eventually, to lay their eggs and look after their chicks.

AMAZING JOURNEYS

The wandering albatross laughs in the face of long distances! It can:

- fly over 1,000km in a single day.
- make 10,000km feeding trips in 10-20 days.
- One albatross was tracked flying all the way around Antarctica in just 46 days.
- As they can live for 80 years, a wandering albatross flies many millions of kilometres in its lifetime.

MAXIMUM SIZE: 3.7m wingspan **MAXIMUM WEIGHT:** 13kg **FOUND IN:** The Southern Ocean, around Antarctica **CREATURE FEATURE:** The wandering albatross has a huge hooked beak, which it can make white or pink by controlling the way blood flows through it.

WONDER WINGS
The albatross's amazing wings let it swoop close to the ocean, soar up again, and stay at sea for years.

DID YOU KNOW?
Some sailors used to believe that albatrosses protected seafarers, and killing one was very bad luck. However, that didn't stop people from catching and eating them, using their bones to make flutes, and their feet to make little bags!

OSTRICH

The biggest bird on Earth is so huge and heavy, it can't get off the ground. But if that conjures up a vision of a helpless, waddling lump – think again! Ostriches are fast, fierce and and furious. They can run fast enough and kick hard enough to defend themselves from all kinds of dangerous enemies, like lions, wild dogs and hyenas.

For a human, an encounter with an ostrich can be quite scary – they can stand an astonishing 2.7m tall (tall enough to hit their heads on the ceiling in most houses) and weigh more than twice as much as a human.

RECORD RUNNER

The ostrich isn't just the biggest and tallest, but also the fastest-running bird. It can sprint across the plains on its long legs at speeds of 70km/h. One massive male ostrich even chased a speeding truck full of wildlife-watchers after it came too close to him.

DID YOU KNOW?

In prehistoric times, there used to be birds similar to ostriches but even bigger, like the giant moa of New Zealand. It could reach 3.5m tall, and weighed 400kg.

MAXIMUM SIZE: 2.75m tall **MAXIMUM WEIGHT:** 150kg **FOUND IN:** Dry areas and grasslands in Africa **CREATURE FEATURE:** The ostrich has only two toes on each foot, one with an enormous, sharp, sturdy killer claw.

NEEEEOOW!
An ostrich sprinting at full speed can easily outrun the fastest human athletes.

RECORD EGG

The ostrich also holds the record for laying the biggest eggs of any living bird. They are about 15cm long and weigh 1.4 kg, as much as 24 chicken eggs. In many countries, ostriches are farmed for their meat and eggs, as chickens are. Their eggs taste like chicken's eggs but take 90 minutes to boil!

KEEP AWAY!
Nobody's going to be eating these ostrich eggs, as the mother is defending them fiercely.

GIANT WETA

The Little Barrier Island giant weta is the heaviest insect on earth. This monster insect is so big, it thinks nothing of gobbling up a whole carrot, and fills the palm of a man's hand. A weta is a grasshopper-like insect, and the largest ones, like this, cannot fly. They just crawl around slowly, feeding mostly on fruit and seeds. If danger threatens, they can bite to defend themselves, or scratch their enemies with their prickly legs.

However, wetas are usually quite mild-mannered and not dangerous to humans. Many people in New Zealand, where they are found, are happy to pose for a photo with an enormous weta crawling across their arm or even their face!

FOREST DWELLER
A giant weta at home in its natural habitat, on tree bark in a New Zealand forest.

MIND THOSE CLAWS!
Wetas are friendly and quite happy to sit in your hand, though their sharp claws can be a bit scratchy.

MAXIMUM SIZE: 10cm body length Maximum weight: 70g **FOUND IN:** Islands off New Zealand **CREATURE FEATURE:** Females seem to have a nasty-looking sting, but it's actually an ovipositor, a tube for laying eggs.

ISLAND GIANTS

The biggest giant wetas can have a body 10cm long, a legspan of 20cm, and weigh as much as 70g – three times as much as a mouse. In fact, on the islands where they live, there aren't any small mammals like rats, and wetas take their place, eating similar foods. Without these animals to hunt them, and with plenty of food around, they can become enormous. For similar reasons, many islands around the world have animal giants living on them.

DID YOU KNOW? The scientific name for giant wetas is Deinacrida, meaning 'terrible grasshopper'!

GOLIATH BEETLE

Imagine this flying past your face on a stroll through the jungle! The aptly named Goliath beetles are the biggest of all beetles by weight, and the heaviest insects that can fly, at up to about 60g. Their head and body length can be almost 12cm, which is longer than your hand, and their wings when spread out wide can measure 25cm. Aaargghh!

HEAVY HANDFUL
A brightly coloured Goliath beetle stops for a rest on someone's outstretched hand.

MAXIMUM SIZE: 12cm long **MAXIMUM WEIGHT:** 60g **FOUND IN:** Central African rainforests **CREATURE FEATURE:** Males have Y-shaped horns, used mainly for battling other males.

MONSTER MAGGOT

The adult beetle holds the record for heaviest flying insect, but the larva or maggot, the baby beetle, doesn't fly and can grow even bigger. In just a few months after hatching out of its egg, it becomes a fat, spotted, 12cm-long wriggling sausage weighing up to 100g, as much as a small banana. It loses weight after becoming a pupa and transforming itself into a fully grown beetle.

LOOK OUT!
With its wings opened out for flight, a Goliath beetle could be wider than your head!

DID YOU KNOW?
As it zooms around in the forests of central Africa, the Goliath beetle's massive buzzing wings make a noise that's said to sound like a small helicopter!

QUEEN ALEXANDRA'S BIRDWING

If you took a female Queen Alexandra's birdwing butterfly and spread it out on a dinner plate, its wings would reach right over the sides! This huge butterfly's wingspan can reach over 30cm across – and the male is almost as wide, though his wings are narrower.

BRIGHT BUTTERFLY
The male birdwing has striking bright green and black markings.

MAXIMUM SIZE: 31cm wingspan **MAXIMUM HEAD AND BODY LENGTH:** 8cm **FOUND IN:** Forests in parts of Papua New Guinea **CREATURE FEATURE:** The enormous female has a patch of bright red fur on her body.

DON'T EAT ME!

You probably wouldn't ever put this butterfly on a plate, because it would taste foul. Both the adult butterflies are brightly coloured, and so is the spiky, scary-looking caterpillar – a sign that they are all poisonous and revolting to eat, in order to put off predators. The birdwing becomes poisonous by feeding on a type of poisonous vine, both as a caterpillar and as a butterfly. The poison doesn't affect it, but builds up in its body.

MALE OR FEMALE?
Females are a bit bigger and mainly brown, with a brighter underside.

DID YOU KNOW?

The first explorer to discover this butterfly was an English naturalist, A. S. Meek, in 1906. He actually shot one of the butterflies with a gun! He then collected it and sent it back to England, where the species was named after the English queen at the time.

FLATTENED FORESTS

The Queen Alexandra's birdwing is found only in a small, forested area of Papua New Guinea in south east Asia. A large area of its habitat has been turned into farmland, and even more was destroyed by a volcanic eruption in 1951. So the birdwing is now rare and endangered.

TARANTULA HAWK WASP

Just beating the Asian giant hornet for the title of world's biggest wasp is the tarantula hawk wasp. With their long, dangly legs and black bodies, tarantula hawks look more fly-like than wasp-like. However, they are definitely wasps, and have one of the insect world's most painful stings. It's said to feel like a sudden electric shock that's so agonizing, you can't think about anything else except screaming! Luckily, the pain only lasts three minutes.

AARRGH! GET OFF!
Despite its eight legs, fangs and prickly hairs, it's hard for a tarantula to avoid the tarantula hawk's sting.

MAXIMUM SIZE: 7cm long **MAXIMUM WINGSPAN:** 11cm **FOUND IN:** Many warmer parts of the world, wherever there are tarantulas. **CREATURE FEATURE:** A powerful, 7mm-long sting.

RED WASP
Tarantula hawk wasps come in a variety of colours.

TARANTULA KILLER

The tarantula hawk wasp gets its name because it mercilessly hunts and attacks tarantulas, even those that are much bigger than itself. Adult wasps don't eat tarantulas: they prefer plant nectar. Instead, female wasps catch tarantulas to use as baby food. After sniffing out a tarantula, the wasp flips it over, avoiding its struggling legs, and stings it in the side or underside. The wasp's venom doesn't kill the spider, but paralyzes it permanently. Then the wasp lays an egg on the spider, and buries it safely underground. When the egg hatches, the larva feeds on the still-living spider, eventually eating it all up from the inside out.

DID YOU KNOW?

As the wasp larva feeds on the tarantula, it somehow knows how to avoid the spider's main organs, keeping it alive and fresh for as long as possible.

GOLIATH BIRD-EATING SPIDER

You've met the Goliath frog and the Goliath beetle. Now for the scariest of them all – the Goliath bird-eating spider, or Goliath birdeater. Its name gives you a few clues about what this creature is – an absolutely massive, hairy, muscly tarantula that's so big it can eat a bird (or a mouse, a frog, a small snake or even a bat!). It's the biggest of all spiders, with a legspan of up to 30cm, and venomous fangs 2.5cm long.

GRUMPY GOLIATH

The Goliath spider's bite isn't deadly to humans, but it does hurt and can make you feel ill. If you ever do get close to one of these super-spiders, take care, because they are easily annoyed. An angry birdeater will rear up and wave its front legs, rub its leg bristles together to make a hissing sound, and flick itchy hairs at you, before striking and sinking in its teeth. It also uses its bite to kill its prey, before dragging it off to eat in its underground burrow.

SPIDERS AT HOME
Luckily, bird-eating spiders don't like living in human homes – apart from those that are kept as pets!

MAXIMUM SIZE: 30cm legspan **MAXIMUM WEIGHT:** 170g **FOUND IN:** Rainforests in the far north of South America. **CREATURE FEATURE:** Its thick covering of hair, which it can shed and fling at enemies.

SPIDER OF NIGHTMARES
If you're scared of spiders, just a photo of this one will probably give you the heebie-jeebies. It looks like something from as horror film, or even a huge hairy joke spider.

DID YOU KNOW?
Animal giant are sometimes given the name Goliath after a famous human giant described in several ancient writings. He wasn't as huge as you might think, though – only about 2m tall, which is taller than average but certainly possible for a human.

GIANT EARTHWORM

When we normally encounter earthworms, burrowing through the soil or wriggling out of the ground after a rainstorm, they are slimy, squishy and creepy-crawly but usually quite small – no bigger than a pencil. But imagine a worm 30 times that size! Giant earthworms really do exist, and not just in strange sci-fi films – but because they like to stay underground, they are rarely seen.

THE GIANT OF GIPPSLAND

Gippsland in southern Australia is home to one of these mysterious monster worms. The giant Gippsland earthworm likes very wet conditions, and burrows along in soggy tunnels half-filled with water. It hardly ever appears above ground, but you can sometimes spot its 7cm-long cocoons with baby worms wriggling inside, waiting to hatch. The worm itself has been measured at up to 3m long.

MYSTERIOUS MONSTERS
The worms in these photos are fairly large, but it's very hard to take a photo of the biggest earthworms of all, as they are so good at hiding.

MONSTER WORM RECORD

The most monstrous worm discovered so far, however, Is the giant earthworm of South Africa. One individual, discovered in 1967, is said to have measured almost 7m long. Very little is known about these worms, and it's possible there could be even bigger ones lurking beneath the ground.

MAXIMUM SIZE: 6.7m long Maximum width: 2-3cm **FOUND IN:** South Africa and Gippsland, Australia **CREATURE FEATURE:** Incredibly stretchy (which can make them difficult to measure)

DID YOU KNOW?
As the giant Gippsland earthworm squelches through its tunnels, it makes a bizarre gurgling, squirting sound, which is very useful for helping scientists to track it down to study it.

GIANT AFRICAN LAND SNAIL

A giant African land snail's shell can grow to 27cm long, with the snail inside, when it comes out, being even longer. Their huge size aside, they look very like the much smaller garden snails you come across on plants and walls. Like them, they feed on plant food, especially crops, making them a nightmare for farmers.

PET SNAILS

The giant snail is also a popular pet in many parts of the world, although some countries have banned it because of the risk of escaped snails destroying precious crops. Pet snail owners prize them for their size and beautiful markings, which come in lots of different patterns. Some say that with their shells, slow speed and leaf-munching habits, they make a similar pet to a tortoise.

RECORD SNAIL
There are several giant African land snail species – this one, the tiger snail, is one of the biggest.

MAXIMUM SIZE: 27cm shell length **MAXIMUM WEIGHT:** 900g
FOUND IN: Forests and leafy areas in Africa
CREATURE FEATURE: A massive, smooth, cone-shaped shell with stripes, zigzags or mottled markings.

OUT OF THE WATER

Most land snails don't grow this big, because it's hard to carry an enormous shell around on land. Land snails have quite thin shells too, as if they were really thick and strong, they would be too heavy to hold up. In the sea, it's a different story, as the water supports sea creatures and they can be bigger and heavier. Some sea snails, like the giant whelk, can have shells up to 70cm long.

MUNCH!
Pet giant African land snails tuck into salad for lunch. These snails love all kinds of plant food, including the juicy strawberry below.

DID YOU KNOW?
Just as some people eat smaller snails, these giant ones are also popular as a food, especially in African cooking.

CHAN'S MEGASTICK

Stick insects are hard to spot, even if they're enormous, thanks to their amazing resemblance to green twigs. It helps them to avoid being eaten by predators in the trees and bushes where they live.

So there are probably many stick insect species we haven't yet discovered, and scientists often find new ones. This one, called Chan's megastick, was only properly measured and given a scientific name in 2008. It now holds the title of world's longest insect. If you just measure its head and body, it's 35.7cm long. With its front legs stretched out above its head, it reaches to 56.6cm. You can see how big that is in the photo on this page!

WHO IS CHAN?

Chan's megastick was named after Malaysian naturalist Datuk Chan Chew Lun. He didn't discover the stick insect in the wild, but was given a dead one by a local farmer in Borneo. When he saw how huge it was, he knew it must be a record-breaker and donated it to the Natural History Museum in London, UK, which keeps huge collections of wildlife specimens. When it got its Latin name, scientists chose *Phoebaticus chani*, with Chan's megastick as the common name.

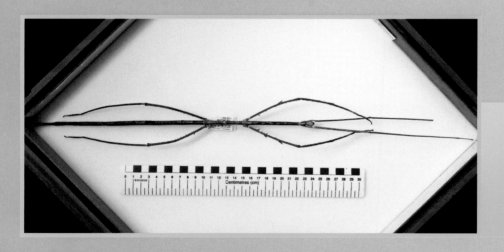

RECORD BREAKER
This is Chan's original megastick, now kept in the Natural History Museum in London, UK.

MAXIMUM SIZE (NOT INCLUDING LEGS): 35.7cm long **MAXIMUM SIZE (INCLUDING LEGS):** 56.7cm long **FOUND IN:** Forests in Sabah, part of Malaysia on the island of Borneo **CREATURE FEATURE:** The shape, colour and texture of its body and legs, are exactly like plant stalks.

DID YOU KNOW?

The female insect given to Chan contained eggs, and scientists were amazed to find each egg had tiny flaps on it, like wings. As the megastick lives high in the treetops, these flaps probably work like the wings found on some seeds, helping the eggs to get carried away by the wind and hatch in another area.

MASTER OF DISGUISE
Even a huge stick insect like this can easily hide in a tree or bush, blending in brilliantly with its surroundings.

ROBBER CRAB

Bumping into this ginormous crab could really give you a fright – especially as it isn't a sea creature, but walks around on land. In the tropical islands where it lives, it could be sitting in a tree above your head, or might even try to raid your dustbin! It's called the robber crab, and is amazing to look at, with its brightly patterned shell in shades of blue, purple, orange or red. Its body can be as big as a beach ball, and its legs up to 1m across.

NIP NIP!
Robber crabs sometimes nip people with their giant pincers. Locals say tickling the crab's tummy makes it let go!

MAXIMUM SIZE: 1m legspan **MAXIMUM WEIGHT:** 4.1kg **FOUND IN:** Islands in the Pacific and Indian Oceans. **CREATURE FEATURE:** Giant front pincers for breaking open nuts.

MONSTER MUNCHER

The robber crab is also called the coconut crab, as it likes coconuts. It sometimes climbs up palm trees to get them, and is strong enough to open a coconut shell with its claws. However, it eats all kinds of other things too, including fruit, other crabs, and carrion or dead meat. It uses its brilliant sense of smell to track down a snack, can easily climb up trees and buildings, and can lift objects much heavier than itself, sometimes stealing food and other items from people's houses.

LUNCH IS SERVED
A robber crab gets to grips with a fresh coconut, one of its favourite snacks.

DID YOU KNOW?

Like other crabs, the robber crab does lay its eggs in the sea, but after only a few weeks, the babies come ashore and spend the rest of their lives on land. As adults, robber crabs can only breathe air, and drown if they go underwater.

WHERE IN THE WORLD?

Use this world map to see at a glance where the animal giants in this book can be found in the wild.

Key:

- African elephant
- Rhinoceros
- Hippopotamus
- Flying fox
- Polar bear
- Tiger
- Giraffe
- Gorilla
- Blue whale
- Sperm whale
- Elephant seal
- Whale shark
- Great white shark
- Ocean sunfish
- Giant octopus
- Giant and colossal squid
- Japanese spider crab
- Lion's mane jellyfish
- Leatherback turtle
- Giant isopod
- Bootlace worm
- Green anaconda
- King cobra
- Saltwater crocodile
- Giant tortoise
- Komodo dragon

- Chinese giant salamander
- Goliath frog
- Andean condor
- Wandering albatross
- Ostrich
- Emperor penguin
- Giant weta
- Goliath beetle
- Queen Alexandra's birdwing butterfly
- Asian giant hornet
- Tarantula hawk wasp
- Goliath bird-eating spider
- Giant earthworm
- Giant African land snail
- Chan's megastick
- Robber crab

GLOSSARY

allergy Extreme body reaction to venom or another substance, which can make you very ill.

amphibian Type of animal that lives in and out of water, such as frogs and toads.

arthropod Type of animal with jointed legs, including insects, spiders and crabs.

bacteria Tiny living things that can sometimes cause diseases.

blowhole Hole in a whale's or dolphin's head, used for breathing through.

blubber Layer of fat found under the skin of sea animals such as whales.

breach To leap up out of the water and then splash into it again.

captive Kept in a zoo, cage or other enclosure.

carnivore Animal that hunts and eats meat.

carrion Old, rotting meat from an animal that has already died.

colony A group of animals, such as ants, that live and work together.

constrictor A snake that kills its prey by squeezing it to death.

crustacean A type of animal with jointed legs and a tough shell, such as crabs and shrimps.

delicacy Something considered valuable and delicious to eat.

echolocation A way of sensing the surroundings by bouncing sounds off them.

endangered In danger of dying out and becoming extinct.

exoskeleton A hard or tough outer shell that some animals have instead of bones.

extinct No longer existing.

filter-feeder Animal that sieves the water around it to catch small pieces of food.

flare A type of firework that makes a bright light to act as a warning or signal.

gills Organs used by some animals, such as fish, to breathe underwater.

kraken A mythical sea monster that was said to resemble a giant octopus.

krill Small shrimp-like creatures which many sea creatures rely on as food.

larva The young of some types of animals, such as insects.

liger A cross between a lion and a tiger.

nectar Sweet liquid made by flowers.

plankton Tiny plants and animals that float around freely in seawater.

predator Animal that hunts and eats other animals.

prehistoric From the time before people wrote down historical records.

prey Animal that is hunted and eaten by another animal.

pupa A life cycle stage in some insects, in which they change from a larva to an adult.

scavenger Animal that feeds on leftovers and carrion rather than killing its own prey.

snorkel Tube used for breathing underwater.

social animals Animals that like to live in groups and do everything together.

spermaceti Large organ in the head of a sperm whale, and also the waxy substance inside it.

suckers Round, rubbery disks that octopuses and squid have for gripping onto objects.

tentacles Long, bendy limb or body part, such as those found on squid.

venom Poisonous substance that a creature injects into its prey or enemies.

venomous Able to inject venom, using a sting, fangs or spines.

vibrate To shake quickly to and fro.

INDEX